About this Book

The "original" **Love-U-Grams** are very popular! So, we've come up with more thoughtful ways to connect with the kids in your life.

Awards – Did your son or daughter set the table without asking? Help a younger sibling get dressed? Or, would you simply like to acknowledge a child's unique individuality? Our awards and certificates give kids an emotional boost and a tangible reminder of how much they're loved.

Lunch Notes – More cute notes for you to tuck in a lunch bag, back pack – or to leave atop a pancake at breakfast! (We've included some cards with no words for the pre-reader set!)

Postcards – These postcards deliver love AND an activity! Kids can color a fun picture, solve a riddle, or complete a word find. Mail them from work or from the mailbox down the street.

Coupons – More ways to make the everyday special. Hand these out as a reward, a pick-me-up or just because you love them so!

More Love-U-Grams

This book is part of the **I Love You So...** product collection, written and illustrated by Marianne Richmond.

Marianne Richmond Studios, Inc.
420 N. 5th Street, Suite 840
Minneapolis, MN 55401
www.mariannerichmond.com

ISBN 0-9774651-0-1

Text and illustrations by Marianne Richmond

Book design by Meg Anderson

Printed in China

First Printing

Award/Certificate

AWESOME KID AWARD

This is to certify that

_____

is a super duper kid, and I love you
just the way you are!

Big Hug _____ date _____

I CAUGHT YOU

_____

being a terrific kid!

Thanks for being you!

Love,_____ date _____

Terrific Helper Award

This award is presented to

_____

for being such a wonderful helper!
I appreciate when you take
the time to help me. I'm really
thankful for you!

Love,_____ date _____

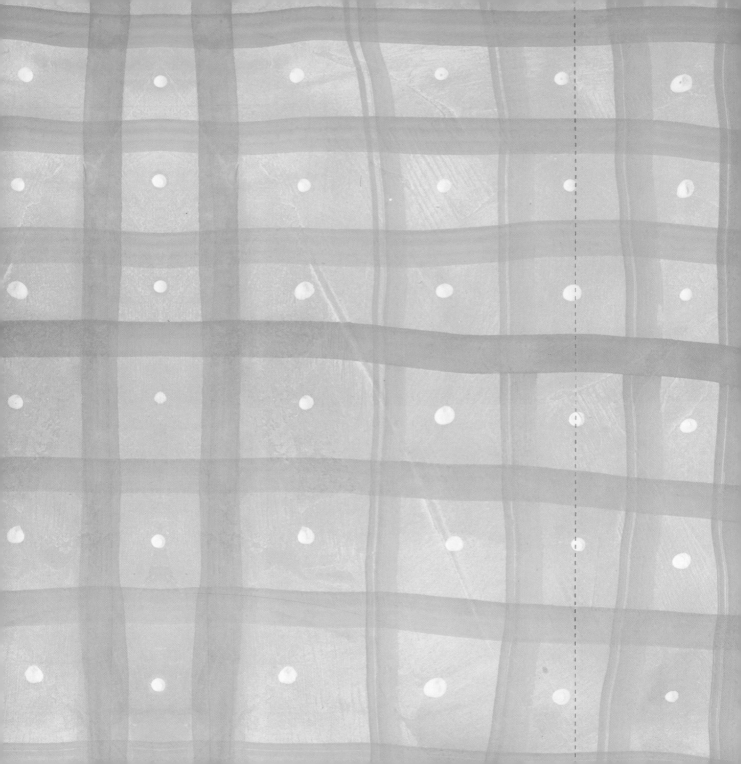

AWESOME KID AWARD

This is to certify that

_____

is a super duper kid,
and I love you just the
way you are!

Big Hug _____ date

Super Son Award

This award is presented to

_____

for being such a super son!
How did I get so lucky to have the gift
of you in my life? I appreciate you!

Love, _____ date _____

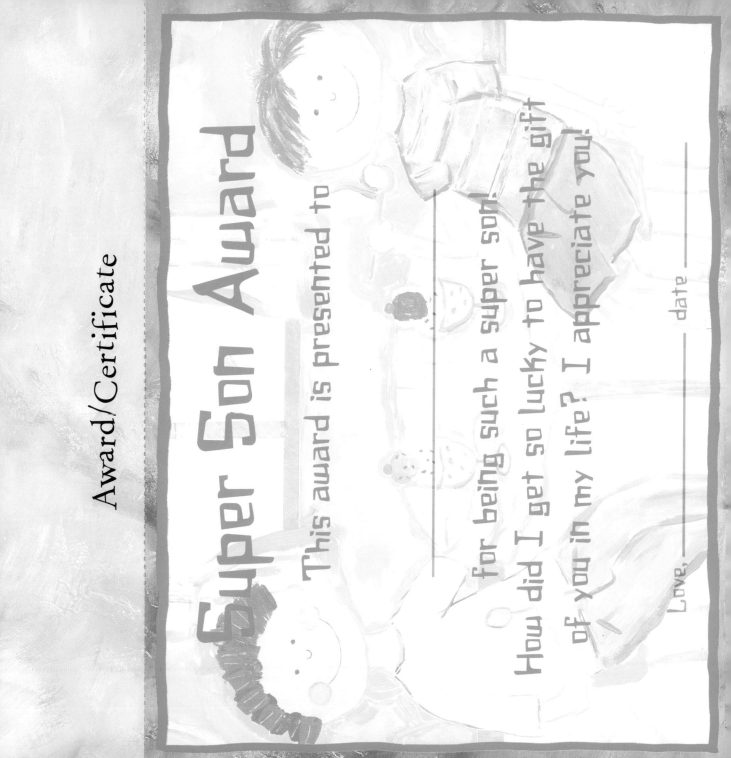

Super Son Award

This award is presented to

_____

For being such a super son!

How did I get so lucky to have the gift
of you in my life? I appreciate you!

Love, _____

_____ date

Delightful Daughter Award

This award is presented to

_____

for being such a delightful daughter!
How did I get so lucky to have the gift
of you in my life? I appreciate you!

Love, _____

date _____

Award/Certificate

Delightful Daughter Award

This award is presented to

_____

for being such a delightful daughter!
How did I get so lucky to have the gift
of you in my life? I appreciate you!

Love, _____ date _____

Lunch Notes

Lunch Notes

Lunch Notes

Hello Sunshine!

You're Special

Love You Bunches

Share your smile with someone who needs it

Lunch Notes

Postcards

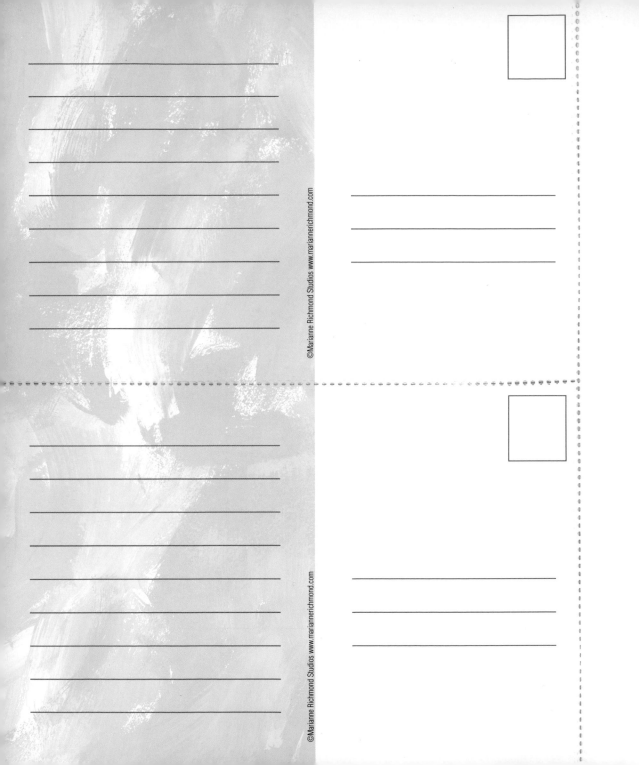

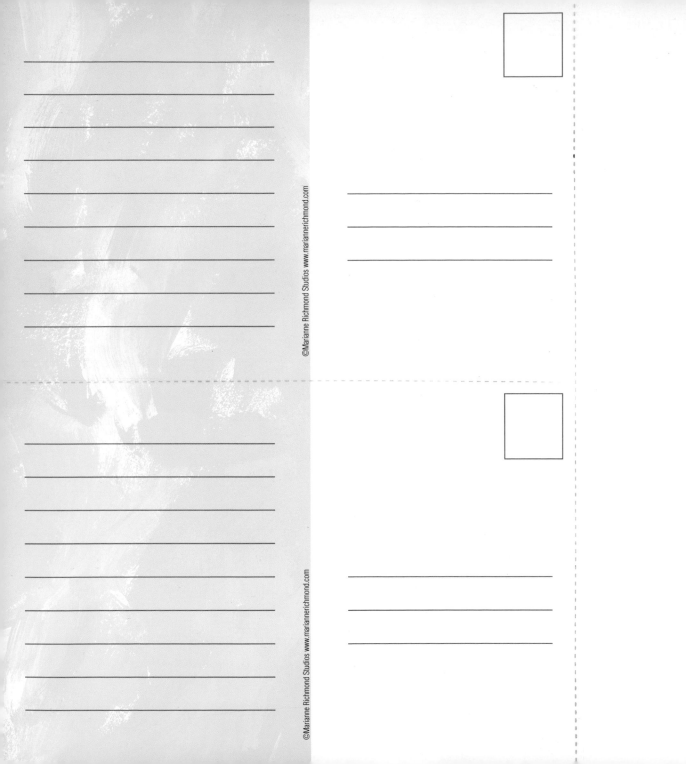

Postcards

Draw lines to connect the matching fish, then color them in.

How many of each fruit are there?

Look at the postcard for one minute. Then turn it over and see how many different shoes you can remember.

Draw in the rest of the picture and color it in.

Postcards

Kid "Coupons"

This coupon is good for one special meal prepared just for you

This coupon is good for $5 cash to spend any way you'd like

THIS COUPON
IS GOOD FOR AN
AFTERNOON
BIKE RIDE

Kid "Coupons"

This coupon is
good for an
outdoor activity
of your choice